Notes for adults:

All recipes require adult supervision. An adult must decide which parts of a recipe a child can do based on their age, ability and the risk involved. Children must be warned not to touch knives, and sharp or hot equipment.

The recipes are ideal for beginners, but some are more of a challenge. The recipes are a guide: ovens and equipment can impact your results.

Little Brother Books Limited is not responsible for adverse reactions, effects or consequences resulting from the use of any recipes or suggestions herein or procedures undertaken hereafter.

CONTENTS

HELLO!

Welcome to a year of fabulous baking. There are lots of recipes and ideas to try, but before you start be prepared:

Safety first

Always cook with an adult. Give them all the jobs that need a knife, such as cutting or slicing. They will also need to look after hot things in the oven or on the hob. They will also need to look after hot things in the oven or on the hob, and be careful not to touch anything hot or sharp. You can have fun planning, shopping, measuring, spooning, stirring, mixing, dividing, shaping, kneading, greasing, decorating and watching the magic happen!

Make with an adult

Get organised

Before you begin, read the whole recipe with your adult chef partner so you can make sure you have enough time, ingredients and utensils. Clear your kitchen of clutter and clean and dry your work surface and equipment. Measure ingredients carefully on accurate scales for best results.

Ingredients

Make sure you have all your ingredients before starting.

Practise

Sometimes things don't always turn out the way you expect. Ovens and equipment are different in every kitchen, so tweak the recipe for next time and try again.

Relax

Baking often involves waiting for the oven to do the hard work. Have fun completing the other activities in this book while your creations are cooking.

Share

Friends make life sweeter – share your bakes with pals or give them out as gifts. Just be sure to check if anyone has an allergy.

Don't forget your oven gloves!

Wash your hands before you start.

STEP INTO SPRING

When the days become brighter and longer you can't help but wake up and smile. Spring is a season filled with energy – everything shoots and suddenly bursts into life!

Put the colour of fresh sunshine into your baking with a special banana breakfast (*page 7*) and an easy pineapple cake (*page 16*).

Cook up some delicious gifts for Valentine's Day (*page 8*), Mother's Day (*page 10*) and Easter (*page 17*), and try the recipes for amazing spring veg too!

BAKED BANANA AND HONEY YOGHURT

A heavenly breakfast, perfect for a spring weekend. Take your pot into the garden and soak up the sunshine!

Serves 2

♥ 2 bananas
♥ a sprinkle of cinnamon
♥ 6 tsp honey (or more to taste)
♥ 200g Greek yoghurt

Extra special: Stir a few drops of vanilla extract into the yoghurt or pop some roasted nuts or raisins on top.

1. Pre-heat the oven to 190ºC/170ºC fan/gas 5. Slice the bananas lengthways, and place on a lightly greased, non-stick baking tray.

2. Drizzle a teaspoon of honey over each banana and sprinkle with cinnamon. Bake for 10–15 minutes until soft and sticky. Rest for 5 minutes.

3. Put a large spoonful of banana at the bottom of two jars. Add a large spoonful of yoghurt. Drizzle a little bit of honey. Continue layering the banana, yoghurt and honey until you run out.

SWEETHEART ♥ PIZZA

Share this lovely treat with your favourite person on Valentine's Day. Love to be together.

Makes 1

- ♥ 1 pack ready-rolled puff pastry
- ♥ 200g chocolate spread
- ♥ 50g pomegranate seeds

1. Pre-heat the oven to 200ºC/180ºC fan/gas 6. Unroll the pastry on a large chopping board.

Top tip: Look for pomegranate seeds in the frozen aisle of a supermarket if you can't find fresh ones.

2. Gently use your finger to draw a large heart. Ask an adult to cut out the shape with a knife and score another heart shape about 2cm from the edge to make a border. Prick the pastry all over with a fork.

Extra special: Drizzle melted white chocolate over the chocolate spread in a pretty pattern.

3. Place the heart on a lightly greased, non-stick baking tray. Bake for 15 minutes, until golden. Leave to cool.

4. Cover the heart with chocolate spread, inside the border, and decorate with pomegranate seeds.

CLUFF / PINK PANCAKES

These airy pancakes are the colours of spring blossom. Just add marshmallows and giggles!

Makes 12 pancakes

- ♥ 200g self-raising flour
- ♥ 1 tsp bicarbonate of soda
- ♥ 50g caster sugar
- ♥ 1 egg
- ♥ 50g butter, melted
- ♥ 250ml milk
- ♥ 125g cottage cheese
- ♥ pink food colouring
- ♥ butter or vegetable oil for frying
- ♥ mini marshmallows

Barbie

1. Pre-heat the oven to 140°C/120°C fan/gas 1.

2. In a bowl, mix together the flour, bicarbonate of soda and sugar. In a separate bowl mix the egg, butter, milk and cottage cheese. Put the two mixtures together and beat well to create a batter.

3. Divide the batter into three bowls. Add 10 drops of food colouring to one bowl, 4 drops to the next bowl and no drops to the last bowl. Mix in the colouring and add more if you want to.

4. Heat a non-stick frying pan over a medium heat. Lightly grease with butter or vegetable oil. Ladle the batter into the pan. Cook each pancake for 1–2 minutes, until bubbles appear on the surface. Flip over and cook for another 30 seconds. Keep the pancakes warm on a tray in the oven while you finish making all of them.

5. Put two handfuls of mini marshmallows in a microwave-safe container. Heat for 30 seconds and mix in 2 teaspoons of water to make a sauce.

6. Stack the pancakes from dark pink to light pink, with the lightest side facing up. Pour over the marshmallow sauce and sprinkle more mini marshmallows on top!

Happy Notes

Sometimes it's small moments that mean the most. Make notes of the things that make you smile on this page.

Send kind ♥r funny notes to your friends and make their day.

BE kind,
BE happy,
BE silly,
BE y♡u!

BROCCOLI PASTA BAKE

Make an all-in-one dinner with your family.

Serves 6

- ♥ 500g dried pasta tubes
- ♥ 350g broccoli, in small florets
- ♥ 75g butter
- ♥ 75g plain flour
- ♥ 1l milk
- ♥ 1 tsp mustard powder
- ♥ 200g cheddar cheese, grated

1. Cook the pasta following the instructions on the packet. Add the broccoli for the last 2 minutes of cooking. Drain and put in an oven dish.

2. Pre-heat the oven to 200ºC/180ºC fan/gas 6.

3. Melt the butter in a saucepan over a medium heat. Add the flour and stir for 1 minute. Pour in the milk and keep stirring as it warms and thickens, until you have a smooth sauce. Remove from the heat and stir in the mustard powder and three-quarters of the cheese. Pour over the pasta and broccoli.

Barbie

Extra special: Add pieces of cooked chicken to the dish and serve with sprigs of fresh basil.

4. Sprinkle the rest of the cheese on top and bake for 30–40 minutes, so it is golden.

MORE IDEAS FOR SPRING

Green dippers

Cut the woody ends off asparagus spears and wrap a thin strip of bacon along each stem. Bake at 200ºC/180ºC fan/gas 6 until the bacon is crispy. Leave to cool slightly and then dip into soft-boiled eggs. Fab for brunch!

Look out for spring greens in season at the shop.

Gold nuggets

Chop a bag of new potatoes into halves or quarters. Toss with a little olive oil, salt, pepper and chopped fresh rosemary. Roast at 200ºC/180ºC fan/gas 6 for 40 minutes until golden. These make a yummy snack or side dish.

Pink zing

Chop 500g rhubarb into finger-sized pieces and put in an oven dish. Tip 85g caster sugar over the veg. Cover with foil and bake for 20 minutes at 200ºC/180ºC fan/gas 6. Leave to cool slightly and serve with ice cream for a gorgeous dessert.

PICK 'N' MIX

Spring has sprung! Get creative and choose your fresh style. Tick your favourite fashion here.

JEWELLED PINEAPPLE CAKE

This beautiful cake is a classic that's fit for a princess and her friends.

Makes a 23cm cake

- ♥ 6 pineapple rings from a tin, drained
- ♥ 6 glacé cherries
- ♥ 6 tbsp golden syrup
- ♥ 200g self-raising flour
- ♥ 200g sugar
- ♥ 2 tsp baking powder
- ♥ 200g butter
- ♥ 4 eggs
- ♥ 1 tsp vanilla extract

Top Tip:
You can use fresh pineapple too!

1. Pre-heat the oven to 180ºC/160ºC fan/gas 4. Lightly grease a 23cm round cake tin.

2. Put the pineapple rings in the bottom, arranged like a flower. Place a glacé cherry in the centre of each ring. Drizzle the golden syrup around the fruit.

3. In a bowl, mix together all the remaining ingredients. Check there are no lumps. Pour the cake mixture into the tin.

4. Bake for 35–40 minutes. Put a skewer in the centre of the cake – if it comes out clean it is cooked. Leave to stand for 15 minutes, then turn out onto a plate.

Cute Cheesecakes

What a delicious way to celebrate Easter with friends!

Makes 12

for the cake
- ♥ 200g digestive biscuits
- ♥ 100g butter, melted

for the filling
- ♥ 425g cream cheese
- ♥ 115g caster sugar
- ♥ ½ tsp vanilla extract
- ♥ 2 eggs

to decorate
- ♥ white chocolate, grated
- ♥ small chocolate eggs

1. Pre-heat the oven to 180ºC/160ºC fan/gas 4. Lightly grease a 12-hole muffin tray.

2. Put the biscuits in a sandwich bag and crush with a rolling pin, or blitz in a food processor, to make small crumbs. Add the melted butter and mix well. Split the biscuit between the muffin holes and press down to make a base.

3. In a large bowl, mix the cream cheese, sugar and vanilla. Beat the eggs in a separate bowl. Add them to the large bowl a little bit at a time as you stir to combine. Spoon the mixture on top of the biscuit base.

4. Bake for 20–25 minutes. The cakes should still have a little wobble in the middle. Leave the cakes in the tray to cool, then take them out and put in the fridge for 4 hours or overnight.

5. Decorate the cheesecakes with grated chocolate and chocolate eggs.

CRIENDS FOREVER

Find five differences between these two spring pictures of pictures of Barbie and her fab friends.

Barbie

IMAGINE, DREAM, REACH

Today I am a brilliant dancer. If you can dream it, you can be it! Colour in this page and get dreaming!

CILL UP WITH SUMMER

Summer is all about fabulous long days with endless potential for fun with friends. Fruit and vegetables grow full and ripen, filling fields and gardens with tempting tastes.

Be a picnic star with courgette bites (*page 22*), homemade bread (*page 24*) and pitta (*page 25*).

Practise your baking skills on holiday with jammy shortbread (*page 28*) and blueberry pastry (*page 29*), and stay cool with ice-cream cookies (*page 30*) and lush lollies (*page 31*). Love every day!

BEAUTIFUL BERRY SMOOTHIE

Strawberries are the taste of summer. Make this fresh smoothie for breakfast or put it in a bottle when you are on the go.

Serves 2

That means remove the green bits!

- ♥ 10 strawberries, hulled
- ♥ 110ml skimmed milk
- ♥ 120g plain yoghurt
- ♥ 2 tbsp honey
- ♥ a few drops of vanilla extract
- ♥ 6 ice cubes
- ♥ 2 tbsp granola (optional)

1. Put all the ingredients apart from the granola in a blender and blitz.

2. Divide the smoothie between two glasses. Add a spoonful of granola on top of each one.

Extra special: Rest some frozen berries on top for a pretty flourish!

BAKED COURGETTE BITES

Take these mini bites to a summer picnic and they will be gone in a few minutes. They are amazing!

Makes 12

- 200g courgette, grated
- 1 onion, finely chopped
- 50g cheddar cheese, grated
- 50g breadcrumbs
- 2 eggs
- 2 tbsp fresh parsley, finely chopped
- salt and pepper, to taste

Top tip:
If you are not keen on parsley, swap it for basil.

Extra special:
Take a tomato salsa dip to go with the bites

1. Pre-heat the oven to 200ºC/180ºC fan/gas 6. Lightly grease a 12-hole muffin tray.

2. Put the grated courgette in a bowl and sprinkle with a little salt. Leave for 5 minutes, then squeeze out the liquid.

3. In a bowl, combine all the ingredients. Fill the muffin tray holes with the mixture and bake for 15–20 minutes, until golden.

4. Leave for a few minutes to cool in the tray and then cool fully on a wire rack.

MORE IDEAS FOR SUMMER

Crunchy corn

Pre-heat the oven to 200°C/180°C fan/gas 6. Mash butter, garlic and parsley with a sprinkle of salt and pepper. Cut pieces of foil large enough to hold a cob. Place a cob on each piece, top with the mash and seal edges to form parcels. Bake for 30–35 minutes. Experiment with toppings – try pesto or barbecue sauce.

FRESH PEAS, LETTUCES, GREEN BEANS AND CARROTS ARE ALSO IN SEASON.

Rainbow kebabs

Cut summer vegetables into large chunks. Choose different colours such as green and yellow pepper, red onion, tomatoes, aubergine and courgette. In a bowl mix some olive oil, lemon juice and chopped herbs. Coat the veg and carefully push the chunks onto skewers. Bake at 200°C/180°C fan/gas 6 for 15 minutes.

Easy frittata

Pre-heat the oven to 200°C/180°C fan/gas 6. Fry chopped bacon and onion in a non-stick pan. Add chopped summer vegetables and cook through before transferring to an oven dish. Beat 9 eggs with 1 teaspoon of paprika and pour over the veggies. Dot with pieces of feta cheese and bake for 30–35 minutes.

FRUIT TOAST

Homemade bread smells fabulous.
Make a loaf and use it to create fruit
toast snacks over a few days.

Makes 1 loaf

for the bread
- ♥ 500g strong wholewheat,
  white bread or granary flour
- ♥ 7g fast-action dried yeast
- ♥ 1 tsp salt
- ♥ 2 tbsp olive oil
- ♥ 1 tbsp clear honey

for the topping
- ♥ cream cheese
- ♥ peaches and raspberries

1. Mix together the dry ingredients in a large bowl. In a jug combine 300ml hand-hot water with the oil and honey, then stir into the dry ingredients to make a soft dough.

2. Turn the dough out onto a lightly floured surface and knead for 5 minutes, until the dough no longer feels sticky. Add a little more flour if you need it.

T♥p Tip:
Slice the loaf and freeze in a bag to keep it super fresh.

3. Lightly grease a loaf tin and put the dough in it. Put in a large plastic food bag and leave to rise for 1 hour, until the dough has risen to fill the tin and it no longer springs back when you press it with a finger.

4. Heat the oven to 200ºC/180ºC fan/gas 6. Make a few slashes across the top of the loaf with a knife, then bake for 30–35 minutes until the loaf is risen and golden. Tip it out onto a wire rack and tap the base of the bread. If it is hollow it is cooked. Leave to cool.

5. Toast a slice of bread. Spread with cream cheese and top with fruit.

KITTY PITTA

Play with your food and make some purr-fect pittas. Meow!

Makes 6 or 10 (depending on size)

for the pitta
- ♥ 7g fast-action dried yeast
- ♥ 290ml warm water
- ♥ 1 tsp salt
- ♥ 420g plain flour

to assemble
- ♥ cucumber
- ♥ pepper
- ♥ carrot
- ♥ olive

1. In a large bowl, mix the yeast and water and wait for 5 minutes. Add the salt and half the flour and beat to make a batter. Add the rest of the flour and make a rough dough. Knead for 8 minutes until the dough is smooth and elastic. Add more flour if it is too sticky.

2. Tip the dough onto a lightly floured surface and divide into 6 pieces for large pittas or 10 for smaller pittas.

3. Form the dough into balls, then flatten with a rolling pin into 0.5cm thick, even discs. Rest on the floured surface for 30–40 minutes until slightly puffed.

4. Pre-heat the oven to 220°C/200°C fan/gas 7 and lightly grease two non-stick baking trays. Bake the pittas on the trays for 12–14 minutes and then cool on a wire rack.

5. For lunch, cut a pitta in half. Cut the vegetables into shapes and arrange them like a cat face (use the photo as a guide). Serve with hummus.

Top tip: Wrap and store the remaining pittas for two days or pop them in the freezer and eat within three weeks.

LURR / AND FADULOUS

Blissa wants to visit her friend at the vet. Show her the way through the maze.

Start here

No Limits

Dream, believe, do, repeat. You can be a sports coach if you put your mind to it. Which two sport pictures match?

JAM HEARTS

Shortbread is so simple and wonderful. Make with love!

Makes 8 (depending on your cutter size)

- ♥ 160g butter
- ♥ 90g caster sugar
- ♥ 240g plain flour
- ♥ 10g icing sugar
- ♥ strawberry jam

Extra special: Why not try making your own strawberry jam?

1. In a bowl, beat together the butter and 80g caster sugar. Mix in the flour. Tip the mixture onto a lightly floured surface and knead for 5 minutes. Wrap the dough in cling film and rest in the fridge for 15 minutes.

2. Pre-heat the oven to 180°C/160°C fan/gas 4 and lightly grease two baking trays. Roll out the dough so it is about 0.5cm thick.

3. Use a round cookie cutter to stamp out 16 circles. Use a small heart cutter to stamp out the centre from 8 of the circles. Score the cookies like the notches on a clock. Spread out the shapes on the trays and sprinkle with the remaining caster sugar.

4. Bake for 15–20 minutes until golden, then cool on a wire rack. Once cold, dust with icing sugar.

5. Warm some jam in a saucepan on a low heat. Spread it over the full circle biscuits and top with the open heart biscuits.

BUTTERFLY BLUEBERRY PUFFS

Don't worry about making these look the same – different is beautiful.

Makes 12 (depending on your cutter size)

- ♥ 1 pack ready-rolled puff pastry
- ♥ 200g blueberries
- ♥ 1 egg
- ♥ icing sugar

1. Pre-heat the oven to 200ºC/180ºC fan/gas 6. Lightly grease a non-stick baking tray.

2. Unroll the pastry on a chopping board. Use a butterfly cookie cutter to make as many butterflies as you can and place them on the tray.

3. Beat the egg in a bowl and use a brush to wash it over the pastry. Dot blueberries on the butterflies.

4. Bake for 10–15 minutes, until puffed and golden. Leave to cool on a wire rack. Sift icing sugar over the puffs to finish.

ICE CREAM CONFETTI COOKIES

Totally cool cookies that turn into sweet sandwiches.

Makes 8

for the cookies
- ♥ 100g butter, softened
- ♥ 100g brown sugar
- ♥ 1 tbsp golden syrup
- ♥ 150g self-raising flour
- ♥ ½ tsp vanilla extract
- ♥ 50g colourful chocolate buttons

to assemble
- ♥ ice cream
- ♥ edible confetti sprinkles

Top Tip: Eat immediately!

1. Pre-heat the oven to 180°C/160°C fan/gas 4. Lightly grease two non-stick baking trays.

2. In a bowl, beat together the butter, sugar and syrup. Mix in the flour and vanilla, then add the chocolate.

3. Divide the mixture into 16 pieces and use your hands to roll into balls and then squash into cookie shapes. Now place well apart on the trays.

4. Bake for 10 minutes until a pale golden colour, then cool on a wire rack.

5. Shake the confetti sprinkles over a plate. Hold one cookie in your hand, flat-side up, and place a small scoop of ice-cream on it. Put another cookie on top and roll the sandwich in the sprinkles.

LUSH LOLLIES

These lollies have been made with strawberries, but you can use any summer fruit you like or a classic vanilla flavour.

Makes 4

- ♥ 250g strawberries
- ♥ 150ml natural yoghurt
- ♥ 3 tsp honey
- ♥ edible colour sprinkles

1. Whizz the ingredients together in a blender.

2. Divide the mixture between 4 ice-lolly moulds, then pop a stick into each one.

3. Put the ice lollies in the freezer for at least 4 hours or until solid.

4. Use your hands to warm the moulds and take out the lollies. Shake sprinkles all over them and serve.

Top Tip: Swap yoghurt for fruit juice if you prefer.

Barbie

BEACH GAME

Time to play volleyball! One shadow is the same as the picture of Barbie. Can you find it?

A

B

C

D

E

SURF'S UP

Colour this cool action picture with your fave beach colours.

GET COSY IN AUTUMN

By the time autumn comes, we're normally ready for a change. I always look forward to baking recipes full of seasonal comforts from harvestime.

Try making baked porridge (*page 35*) and tomato soup (*page 38*) with your family and share honey buns (*page 36*) and cherry cakes (*page 37*) at school.

There are plenty of Halloween dishes to enjoy, including funny ghost drops (*page 45*) and silly witch fingers (*page 46*).

CHERRY KISS CAKES

Find a yummy pink surprise at the bottom of every cake.

Makes 12

- ♥ 100g self-raising flour
- ♥ 100g caster sugar
- ♥ 100g butter, softened
- ♥ 2 eggs
- ♥ 1 tsp vanilla extract
- ♥ 1 tsp baking powder
- ♥ 1 tin cherries in syrup, drained

1. Pre-heat the oven to 180°C/160°C fan/gas 4. Line a 12-hole muffin tray with cake wrappers.

2. Put all the ingredients apart from the cherries in a large bowl and mix well to make a batter.

3. Drop 2–3 cherries in the centre of each cake wrapper. Spoon the batter over the top, dividing equally between each one.

4. Bake for 12–15 minutes until golden. Cool in the tray for a few minutes and then transfer to a wire rack to cool fully.

EXTRA SPECIAL:

Why not top the cakes with icing? In a bowl beat 140g butter with 140g icing sugar until smooth. Add another 140g icing sugar and a dash of milk, and mix well.

HONEY DEAR DUNS

You'll need an angel cake tin to make these adorable bears. They look really sweet on a table and are great to share.

Makes 6 buns

for the buns
- ♥ 280g bread flour
- ♥ 40g beaten egg (some of the egg to be reserved for egg wash)
- ♥ 1 tsp fast-action dried yeast
- ♥ 1 tbsp clear honey
- ♥ 30g vegetable oil
- ♥ 140ml milk

to decorate
- ♥ chocolate chips
- ♥ icing sugar

1. In a large bowl, mix all the ingredients apart from the milk. Slowly add the milk and make a dough. Tip onto a lightly floured surface and knead for 5 minutes.

2. Cut the dough into 6 equal-size portions. Roll into balls and cover and rest for 20 minutes.

3. Lightly grease and flour an angel cake tin. Now make ears for each bun. Pinch off two small balls of dough from each roll. Re-shape the remaining dough so the buns are round again. Put the small balls on top, to make ears (use the photo as a guide). Place the buns in the tin, so there is space between them. Cover and rest for another 20 minutes.

4. Heat the oven to 180°C/160°C fan/gas 4. Brush egg wash over the dough and bake for 18–20 minutes until lightly browned. Cool in the tin for 10 minutes, then transfer to a wire rack.

5. Mix a small amount of icing sugar and water to make icing. Use this with chocolate chips to finish the faces on the buns.

BAKED APPLE PORRIDGE

A warming start to your autumn day.

Serves 4

for the porridge
- 100g oats
- 100g raisins
- 300ml boiling water
- 2 red apples
- 2 tsp cinnamon
- 1 tbsp honey
- 200ml milk
- 50g pecans (optional)

to assemble
- 1 red apple, sliced
- 1 banana, sliced
- 8 raisins
- 4 raspberries

Barbie

1. Pre-heat the oven to 200ºC/180ºC fan/gas 6. In a large bowl, soak the oats and raisins in the boiling water (*be careful!*) for 10 minutes.

2. Peel and cut the apples into small chunks. Add to the oat bowl along with the cinnamon, honey and milk. Stir together.

3. Pour into an oven dish and scatter the pecans on top. Bake for 20 minutes, until the excess liquid has been absorbed.

4. To assemble, spoon the porridge into bowls and make bunny faces with the fruit (using the photo as a guide).

ROASTED TOMATO SOUP

This is the ultimate comforting supper. Eat from a mug on the sofa or outside around a fire.

Serves 4

- ♥ 2 garlic cloves, unpeeled
- ♥ 1 onion, peeled and cut into wedges
- ♥ 1kg plum tomatoes, quartered
- ♥ 3 tbsp olive oil
- ♥ 1l chicken or vegetable stock
- ♥ large handful of fresh basil

Extra special: Dollop a spoonful of sour cream on top of each soup portion and serve with crunchy bread croutons.

1. Pre-heat the oven to 190°C/170°C fan/gas 5.

2. Place the garlic, onion and tomato pieces cut-side up on a non-stick baking tray. Drizzle with oil and a little salt and pepper. Bake for 1 hour.

3. Snip the ends off the garlic cloves and squeeze the insides into a blender along with the onion, roasted tomatoes and juice from the baking tray. Add the stock and basil and blend until smooth.

Pink slaw

Peel and grate 3 carrots, 1 celeriac and 2 apples. Chop ½ red cabbage and 2 pre-cooked beetroots. Mix in a bowl. Separately, combine 4 tbsp natural yoghurt, 4 tbsp mayonnaise and a splash of apple vinegar, then stir into the vegetables. Eat with roasted chicken or fish.

Fill your fridge with autumn vegetables such as butternut squash.

Cheesy mushrooms

Pre-heat the oven to 200°C/180°C fan/gas 6. Put large mushrooms top-side down on a lightly greased non-stick baking tray. Scatter with cheese and breadcrumbs and bake for 10–15 minutes. Makes a delicious snack!

Special mash

Gorgeous with sausages. Boil sweet potatoes for 20–30 minutes. Drain and mash, then mix with a little milk, butter and maple syrup.

APPLE CRUMDLE

Golden, delicious and easy to make. Simply serve with thick yoghurt, cream, custard or ice-cream.

Serves 4-6

for the filling
- ♥ 600g cooking apples, peeled, cored and cut into small chunks
- ♥ 2 tbsp caster sugar

for the topping
- ♥ 175g plain flour
- ♥ 110g caster sugar
- ♥ 110g cold butter, cut into chunks
- ♥ 1 tbsp demerara sugar

Top tip:
You can also make one crumble in a large dish using the same recipe.

Extra special:
Add a squeeze of orange and some orange zest to the apple filling, and 2 tablespoons of oats to the crumble mixture.

1. Pre-heat the oven to 190°C/170°C fan/gas 5. First make the filling. In a bowl mix together the apple chunks and sugar. Divide into individual baking dishes.

2. Using the same bowl, mix the flour and sugar. Add the butter and rub it and the grains between your fingers until the mixture has a crumb texture.

3. Spoon the topping over the filling and even it out with a fork. Sprinkle with demerara sugar, then bake for 45 minutes or until golden. Let the crumbles stand for 10 minutes before eating as they will be very hot.

RRIGHT FUTURE

Do you LOVE music? Imagine setting the music style for an event or filling the dance floor at a party. Make an awesome playlist and design a poster for your showcase.

MAKE YOUR DJ DREAMS COME TRUE! DREAM, wish, do!

My playlist

- ♥ _____
- ♥ _____
- ♥ _____
- ♥ _____
- ♥ _____
- ♥ _____
- ♥ _____
- ♥ _____
- ♥ _____
- ♥ _____

CAD SNAPS

Which way to the fashion show? Guide Barbie and her friends through the maze.

Start here

HALLOWEEN PIES

Bake these fun monster pies with your family on Halloween eve.

Barbie

Makes 4

- ♥ 2 red onions, cut into wedges
- ♥ 550g butternut squash, cut into small chunks
- ♥ 200g Brussels sprouts, trimmed and quartered
- ♥ 2 tbsp olive oil
- ♥ 200g feta cheese, cubed
- ♥ 1 tsp dried oregano
- ♥ 2 tsp paprika (optional)
- ♥ 1 pack ready-rolled puff pastry
- ♥ 1 egg, beaten
- ♥ 4 black olives, sliced

1. Pre-heat the oven to 200ºC/180ºC fan/gas 6. Put the onions, butternut squash and Brussels sprouts on a non-stick baking tray. Drizzle with the oil and bake for 30 minutes, until tender.

2. In a bowl, gently combine the cooked vegetables, cheese, oregano and paprika (if using). Divide between lightly greased, individual pie dishes and add a tablespoon of water to each one.

3. Unroll the pastry and use a cookie cutter to make 4 lids to fit the pie dishes. Cut 24 slim strips from the extra pastry, which will be the legs.

4. Spread out the pie dishes on a baking tray. Arrange 6 legs around each dish, then top with a lid. Brush the pastry with egg and make a small steam hole in the centre of every pie.

5. Bake for 20–25 minutes until the pastry is puffed and golden. Just before you serve, put two olive slices on each pie so they have eyes!

44

GHOST DROPS

Gorgeous mouthfuls of super sweet meringue are easy to whip up for Halloween parties and trick or treat visitors.

- ♥ 3 egg whites
- ♥ 150g caster sugar
- ♥ icing pen

1. Pre-heat the oven to 120°C/100°C fan/gas 1/2. Line two non-stick baking trays with baking paper.

2. Use an electric mixer to whisk the egg whites until soft peaks form. Gradually add the sugar, a tablespoon at a time, whisking well until the sugar dissolves and stiff, glossy peaks form.

3. Spoon the mixture into a piping bag. Snip the end and pipe small blobs onto the baking trays. Bake for 40 minutes and then cool on a wire rack.

4. Once cold, use the icing pen to draw faces onto the side of each ghost drop.

Extra special:
To create colourful ghosts, brush lines of food colouring on the inside of the piping bag. Carefully turn the bag out and add the meringue.

Top tip:
Draw different faces on the ghosts – it'll make your guests giggle. Don't worry if they are slightly different sizes as it looks better that way.

WITCHES FINGERS

Another eerie treat
for Halloween.

Makes about 30

- ♥ 250g ground almonds
- ♥ 250g icing sugar, sifted
- ♥ 2 egg whites, lightly whisked
- ♥ 1 tsp almond extract
- ♥ 100g whole almonds

1. Place the ground almonds and icing sugar in a bowl. Add the egg whites and almond extract and mix well to make a dough. You can use an electric mixer if you have one. Cover the dough and chill in the fridge for 1 hour.

2. Pre-heat the oven to 200ºC/180ºC fan/gas 6. Lightly grease a non-stick baking tray and lightly flour a surface. Scoop a heaped tablespoon of dough and make a sausage shape. Gently press the sausage to turn it into a knuckly finger. Use a clean ruler to make lines where you want to. Press a whole almond into the tip. Transfer to the baking tray and make more fingers.

3. Bake the biscuits for 10 minutes until golden brown and cool on a wire rack.

Top tip: You can dip these almond biscuits into a hot chocolate.

SPOOKY STORY

Dream up a strange tale to share with friends while you enjoy some of your Halloween bakes together.

WARM UP DURING WINTER

During the shortest days full of frost, spend some of your winter weekends warming up in the kitchen.

It's the perfect time of year to practise your baking skills, especially for all the gifts you can create for Christmas. Start with a cooked breakfast (page 49) and try your own homemade pasta (page 52).

Then get festive and fill up with spiced granola (page 56), gingerbread (page 57), star biscuits (page 58) and toasted marshmallow treats (page 59).

BREKKIE BASKETS

There is nothing better than a mini cooked breakfast on a chilly winter's day. Ready, set, bake!

Makes 6

- 3 slices of bread
- 12 slices bacon or ham
- ½ red pepper, chopped
- 6 eggs

1. If you are using bacon, fry on a low heat until cooked, but not crispy. Put it on some kitchen towel to absorb the fat and leave to cool. Pre-heat the oven to 200ºC/180ºC fan/gas 6. Grease 6 holes in a muffin tin.

2. Press the bread slices flat with your palm. Use a cookie cutter or glass to cut out 6 circles. Put the bread circles at the bottom of each hole in the tray.

3. Wrap 2 slices of bacon or ham around the sides of each hole. Crack an egg into a small bowl and pour it into a hole and repeat for the others. Top with pepper pieces.

4. Bake for 15–20 minutes until the egg is set. Watch the baskets to make sure the bacon doesn't burn.

Top Tip:

Swap the pepper for mushrooms – simply cook them with the bacon at the beginning. Decorate the baskets with fresh sprigs of herbs and black pepper before serving.

PICK 'N' MIX

Looking cool! Which winter wardrobe pieces do you love the most? Tick your picks.

PERFECT PINK PASTA

Making pasta is really fun, but pink pasta tops them all. This recipe takes a little bit of time so save it for a lazy Sunday.

Serves 4

- ♥ 3 beetroots
- ♥ 400g '00' flour
- ♥ 4 eggs, 3 whole and 1 yolk
- ♥ pinch of salt

Barbie

1. Heat the oven to 180°C/160°C fan/gas 4. Roast the beetroot on a lightly greased, non-stick baking tray for 1 hour. Leave to cool, then peel and slice. Purée with a hand blender or food processor.

2. On a large surface, pour the flour in a mound and make a well in the centre. In a bowl, combine the eggs, salt and 4 tablespoons of purée, then pour into the well. Using the tips of your fingers, mix the ingredients a little at a time, until combined. Add a little more flour from the packet and knead for 10 minutes to get a silky, elastic ball. Wrap tightly in cling film and rest in a cool place for 30 minutes.

3. Cut the dough into 8 pieces. On a lightly floured surface, roll out a piece at a time while keeping the rest of the dough wrapped up. Roll each piece thinly and try to make an oblong shape. Fold and re-roll the pieces to make sheets as thin as a playing card with a silky sheen. Stack with layers of baking paper and cover with some kitchen towel.

4. Roll each pasta sheet like a Swiss roll. Slice into strips and uncurl to see your tagliatelle. Cook in a saucepan of boiling water for 1–2 minutes and drain.

T♥ SERVE: This pasta tastes wonderful with baked meatballs, a dollop of sour cream and a sprinkle of dill. Or just stir in some yummy pesto!

MORE IDEAS FOR WINTER

Tasty parsnips

Pre-heat the oven to 200°C/180°C fan/gas 6. Peel and slice parsnips into fingers and place on a non-stick baking tray. Drizzle with honey and roast for 30 minutes or until golden.

Lovely leeks

Cut 1 leek and 1 cauliflower into chunks and cook in a pan of boiling salted water for 4–5 minutes until just tender. Drain and put in a baking dish. Make a batch of cheesy sauce from page 12 and cover the veg. Sprinkle with grated cheese and bake at 200°C/180°C fan/gas 6 for 30 minutes.

Fruity flapjack

In a pan over a gentle heat, melt 125g butter, 75g demerara sugar and 2 tablespoons of golden syrup. Peel, core and grate an apple and stir it into the melted ingredients along with 250g oats. Press half the mixture into the bottom of a square baking dish lined with baking paper. Mash 200g blackberries and spoon over the oats to create a layer. Cover with the remaining oats from the pan. Bake at 190°C/170°C fan/gas 5 for 30–40 minutes. Cool and cut into squares.

Cool Fashionistas

Find ten differences between these two winter pictures of the fab friends.

FESTIVE BREAKFAST

Two recipes to start your Christmas with festive flavours. Both will make enough for 4 people.

Christmas tree

- ♥ bag of kiwis
- ♥ Mixed berries – redcurrants, blueberries and raspberries

1. Peel and slice the kiwis into semi-circles. Arrange on plates to make tree pictures, using the photo as a guide.

2. Decorate the trees with the different berries.

Barbie

Reindeer crunch

- ♥ 300g oats
- ♥ 50g mixed nuts
- ♥ 50g mixed seeds
- ♥ 50g caster sugar
- ♥ 4 tbsp vegetable oil
- ♥ 2 tbsp maple or golden syrup
- ♥ ½ tsp ground cinnamon
- ♥ ½ tsp mixed spice
- ♥ ½ tsp ground ginger
- ♥ 100g sultanas
- ♥ 100g dried cranberries
- ♥ 50g chocolate chips

1. Pre-heat the oven to 140°C/120°C fan/gas 1. Apart from the sultanas, cranberries and chocolate, mix the ingredients in a bowl. Spread out on a non-stick baking tray.

2. Bake for 40 minutes and leave to cool. Put the cooked crunch back into the bowl and stir in the sultanas, cranberries and chocolate. This is great to eat while you open some presents!

GINGERDREAD DECORATIONS

Sugar and spice and all things nice, that's what gingerbread is made of. Use a variety of cookie cutters to make different ornaments for Christmas.

Makes 30 depending on the size

- 340g plain flour
- 1½ tsp grated nutmeg
- 1½ tsp ground cloves
- 2 tsp ground cinnamon
- 3 tsp ground ginger
- 1 tsp baking powder
- ½ tsp salt
- 225g butter, softened
- 340g soft brown sugar
- 1 egg, beaten
- 230g icing sugar, sifted

Top tip:
Wait for the icing to dry before threading a piece of ribbon through the hole in each biscuit. Make a loop and knot, then hang on your tree, window or Christmas display.

1. Sift together the flour, spices, baking powder and salt into a large bowl.

2. In another bowl, beat together the butter and sugar. Gradually add the egg and continue to beat. Stir the wet mixture into the flour to make a dough. On a lightly floured surface, roll out the dough so it is as thick as a £1 coin. Put on a tray, cover with cling film and put in the fridge for 30 minutes.

3. Heat the oven to 180°C/160°C fan/gas 4. Use Christmas-themed cookie cutters to make shapes from the dough and place them on a lightly greased, non-stick baking tray. Bake for 10 minutes. Transfer to a wire rack and use a skewer to make a hole at the top of each biscuit. Leave to cool.

4. Mix the icing sugar with a small amount of hot water to make a paste. Separate into bowls and add different food colouring to each one. Fill piping bags and have fun decorating the biscuits! Use the photo to inspire you.

SANTA STARS

These biscuits make cool gifts. Just pop in a food box or bag and wrap with bright ribbon.

Makes about 30

for the biscuits
- 150g plain flour
- 100g butter, cubed
- 75g caster sugar
- 1 unwaxed lemon, washed, zest grated
- 1 egg yolk
- pinch of salt

for the decoration
- 300g icing sugar, sifted
- 3 tsp lemon juice
- red and white sprinkles
- mini marshmallows
- red sweets (chocolate or jelly)
- icing pen

1. Pre-heat the oven to 180°C/160°C fan/gas 4. Put the flour and butter in a bowl. Rub the ingredients between your fingers until you get a breadcrumb texture. You can use an electric mixer to whizz them together if you have one.

2. Add the sugar, lemon zest, egg yolk and salt to the bowl. Mix well, then tip onto a lightly floured surface and form into a ball. Wrap in cling film and put in the freezer for 10 minutes.

3. Lightly flour your surface again and roll the dough so it is the thickness of a £1 coin. Use a star cookie cutter to make shapes and place them on a lightly greased, non-stick baking tray. Chill in the freezer for another 10 minutes. Bake for 15 minutes and cool on a wire rack.

4. Mix the icing sugar with a little hot water to make a paste. Stir in the lemon juice. Apart from a rough circle in the centre, cover the stars with icing and white sprinkles. Use the red sprinkles to make hats and put a mini marshmallow on the top of the hats. Add a red sweet nose to the centre of each star and use the icing pen to dot eyes above.

SNOW FRIENDS

Enjoy these marshmallow pops by gently melting them over a log fire with an adult.

- ♥ 1 bag of marshmallows
- ♥ 50g desiccated coconut
- ♥ 1 packet white candy melts
- ♥ icing pens

1. Soak some bamboo skewers in water for 30 minutes. Prepare the candy melts following the instructions on the packet. Pour the coconut onto a plate.

2. Carefully push a marshmallow onto a skewer. Dip the marshmallow into the white candy, then roll it in the coconut.

3. Push another 2 marshmallows onto the skewer and rest it on a large plate or sheet of baking paper. Repeat to make as many snow friends as you like.

4. Use icing pens to draw faces and arms on the plain marshmallows.

MY NEW YEAR BOARD

Fill this side of the board with photos of sweet memories from last year.

Fill this side of the board with wishes for next year.

LET'S PARTY!

Whether you're planning a tea party, a birthday party or a pyjama party, this section has something tasty for you to try.

Check you are making the right quantity for the number of guests and double or halve if you need to.

TRADITIONAL LEMONADE

Who doesn't love lemonade at a party? Try making your own to go with some of your bakes.

Makes 1 litre

- ♥ 4 unwaxed lemons, washed
- ♥ 100g caster sugar

1. Thinly peel the zest from the lemons with a vegetable peeler. Leave as much pith on the fruit as you can. Put the zest in a large heatproof jug and add juice from the lemons plus the sugar.

2. Add 600ml boiling water (*be careful, ask an adult for help*) and stir until the sugar has all dissolved. Cover and leave to cool completely.

3. Strain the lemon mixture into a serving jug and get rid of the zest. Dilute with 400ml chilled water and sweeten with a little extra sugar if you like.

Barbie

Barbie

Extra special: Decorate your refreshing drink with lemon slices, mint leaves and crushed ice.

MINI BURGERS

This American favourite is really easy and delicious.

Makes 8

for the burgers
- ♥ 1 small onion, chopped
- ♥ 1 small carrot, grated
- ♥ 250g lean beef mince
- ♥ 1 tsp dried mixed herbs
- ♥ 2 tbsp tomato sauce
- ♥ 1 tsp Worcestershire sauce

to assemble
- ♥ 8 small buns
- ♥ 8 leaves of lettuce
- ♥ 8 slices of tomato

Extra special: Add a small square of cheese and a slice of gherkin to each mini burger.

Barbie

1. Pre-heat the oven to 180°C/160°C fan/gas 4 and lightly grease a non-stick baking tray. Put all the ingredients into a large bowl and mix well with your hands.

2. Take a handful of mixture, form into a little burger shape and put it on the tray. Repeat until the bowl is empty. Bake for 15 minutes, turning halfway through.

3. Once cooked, use the picture as a guide to assemble the burgers for serving. Top with a fab relish or mayonnaise.

Top tip: If you prefer, swap the beef for turkey or pork and tomato for an egg.

SMILE / PIZZAS

Have a competition with your guests to see who can decorate a pizza with toppings to make the best smiley face.

Makes 8-12

for the dough
- ♥ 450g strong white bread flour
- ♥ 7g fast-action dried yeast
- ♥ 1 tsp salt
- ♥ 2 tbsp olive oil

for the topping
- ♥ 100ml passata
- ♥ 2 tbsp dried mixed herbs
- ♥ 250g grated mozzarella
- ♥ your choice of sliced ham, salami, chicken, pepper, olives, tomatoes, pineapple, red onion, sweetcorn, grated carrot, spinach, thin broccoli, mushroom, sprigs of rosemary and thyme

Top Tip: Short on time? Grab some pre-made pizza bases from a shop.

1. First make the dough. In a bowl, mix together the flour, yeast and salt. In a jug combine 350ml hand-hot water with the oil and stir the liquid into the dry ingredients to make a wet dough. Set aside for 15 minutes.

2. Turn the dough onto a well-floured surface and gently knead for 2 minutes to make it soft and bouncy, adding more flour if you need to. Put the dough back in the bowl, cover and rest in a warm place for 1 hour.

3. Divide the risen dough into 8 or 12 sections, depending on the pizza size you would like. Roll the sections into balls, then flatten into circles and put them on pieces of foil. Spread a spoonful of passata over each base, sprinkle with dried herbs and give them to guests to top with their own face design.

4. Heat the oven to 240°C/220°C fan/gas 9. Lightly dust non-stick baking sheets with flour. Carefully slide the pizzas onto the sheets and cook for 10–12 minutes until crispy.

SELFIE STICKS

Perfect for selfies and to pop in a party bag to take home. You'll need some cake sticks for this recipe, which are sold in most supermarkets and cake shops.

Barbie

Makes 30

- ♥ 250g plain flour
- ♥ ½ tsp baking powder
- ♥ ½ tsp salt
- ♥ 170g butter, softened
- ♥ 125g caster sugar
- ♥ 1 egg
- ♥ 1 tsp vanilla extract
- ♥ 200g icing sugar
- ♥ food colouring

1. In a bowl, mix together the flour, baking powder and salt. In another bowl cream the butter and sugar until light and fluffy, then mix in the egg and vanilla extract.

2. Add the dry ingredients and stir until everything combines. Wrap the light mixture in cling film and chill for 2 hours.

3. Heat the oven to 160°C/140°C fan/gas 3. On a lightly floured surface, roll out the dough so it is 3mm thick. Cut out shapes with cookie cutters and place on a baking tray lined with baking paper. Position cake sticks on top of the shapes to space them correctly on the tray (with the top of a stick on the centre of a biscuit, pointing down). Then remove the sticks and bake the biscuits for 12–15 minutes. The edges should be lightly browned and the centres pale.

Top tip:

Draw or print the prop shapes on card, cut them out and lay on top of your rolled dough. Ask an adult to cut them out.

4. As soon as you take out the biscuits, gently press the sticks back into position. Allow to cool on the tray for 10 minutes, then transfer to a wire rack to cool fully.

5. Mix the icing sugar with a little warm water to make a paste. Separate into small bowls, use food colouring to colour as you wish and decorate the biscuit props. Use the photo to inspire you!

Extra special: Put in a cake bag or box and tie with a pretty ribbon.

FABULOUS VANILLA CUPCAKES

This is an awesome party recipe. The secret ingredient for the cake and the icing is cream – it makes the cupcakes extra special.

Makes 14

for the cupcakes
- ♥ 165g plain flour
- ♥ 1 heaped tsp baking powder
- ♥ ½ tsp salt
- ♥ 115g butter, softened
- ♥ 200g caster sugar
- ♥ 2 eggs
- ♥ 2 tsp vanilla extract
- ♥ 120g sour cream

for the topping
- ♥ 230g butter, softened
- ♥ 360g icing sugar
- ♥ 2 tsp vanilla extract
- ♥ 30ml double cream
- ♥ pink food colouring
- ♥ edible pink sprinkles

1. Pre-heat the oven to 180°C/160°C fan/gas 4. Line muffin trays with 14 cupcake wrappers.

2. In a bowl combine the flour, baking powder and salt and set aside. In a large bowl, cream the butter and sugar. Add the eggs and vanilla extract and mix well, then pour in the sour cream and mix again. You can use an electric mixer if you have one. Fold in the dry ingredients, 2 spoonfuls at a time.

Extra special:
To pipe a flash of colour in your icing, turn a piping bag inside out and drizzle food colouring in lines, from the tip to the middle or top. Carefully turn it back the right way and position the nozzle, then spoon in the icing as you would normally.

3. Divide the batter between the cupcake wrappers so they are half full. Bake for 18–20 minutes. Put a skewer in the centre of the cakes – if it comes out clean it is cooked. Cool on a wire rack.

4. To make the icing, first beat the butter in a bowl until smooth. Slowly add the icing sugar and continue to mix. Then add the vanilla extract and double cream and stir well until combined.

PRETTY PINK TEA

Surprise your guests with a cup of this delightful rose tea. It goes really well with cupcakes!

Serves 4-6

- Rose bud tea
- 1 unwaxed lemon
- honey or sugar to taste

1. Follow the packet instructions to make the tea in a teapot or a large saucepan.

2. Cut the lemon into thin slices.

3. For each guest, pour a cup of the infusion, add a few rose buds, a slice of lemon and a sprinkle of sugar.

Top Tip:
Find rose tea buds in a tea shop.

ΓIME TO DREAM

Get creative and colour this pattern while you wait for some dough to rise or a cake to cook.

Barbie

l♥VE.

bE y♥u.

BAKING ON THE DRAIN

Can you find all 10 baking items in the word search?

M	Z	R	E	T	N	B	T	Y	R	S	W	O	E	C
K	E	V	E	O	O	O	P	O	C	N	O	L	U	V
D	R	A	R	K	M	W	L	W	Y	O	O	R	M	F
X	Y	P	S	N	A	L	V	Z	C	O	D	B	L	L
V	A	K	D	U	I	C	Z	A	D	P	E	E	K	H
T	C	I	Q	N	R	C	P	Q	B	S	N	D	L	Y
J	S	O	G	I	H	I	I	U	Y	S	H	H	L	L
E	H	P	D	R	Q	T	N	N	C	O	P	C	L	N
F	I	W	H	I	S	K	S	G	G	B	O	K	O	X
N	A	F	I	I	U	U	Z	I	J	C	O	L	S	H
E	P	H	N	R	R	Q	G	N	D	U	N	E	W	E
C	W	K	Z	T	D	J	Y	H	G	U	G	S	H	X
J	R	R	B	A	N	U	Z	U	X	Y	Q	P	K	V
E	U	R	R	V	L	A	B	Z	H	W	S	N	N	A
S	G	E	V	O	L	G	N	E	V	O	I	S	U	A

- ♥ Wooden spoon
- ♥ Apron
- ♥ Oven glove
- ♥ Whisk
- ♥ Measuring jug
- ♥ Spoons
- ♥ Bowl
- ♥ Rolling pin
- ♥ Cupcake
- ♥ Icing

Barbie

MAKE AND BAKE

Stick in photos from your year of baking.
Which recipe do you like the best?

ANSWERS

Page 54-55
Cool fashionistas

Page 73
Baking on the brain

All photographic images used under License from Shutterstock.com